Rookie Read-About® Science

Apples of
Your Eye

By Allan Fowler

Consultants

Robert L. Hillerich, Professor Emeritus,
Bowling Green State University, Bowling Green, Ohio;
Consultant, Pinellas County Schools, Florida

Lynne Kepler, Educational Consultant

Fay Robinson, Child Development Specialist

CHILDRENS PRESS®
CHICAGO

Design by Beth Herman Design Associates
Photo Research by Feldman & Associates, Inc.

Library of Congress Cataloging-in-Publication Data

Fowler, Allan.
    Apples of your eye / by Allan Fowler.
      p. cm. −(Rookie read-about science)
    ISBN 0-516-06026-0
    1. Apples–Juvenile literature. [1. Apples.] I. Title. II. Series.
SB363.F73 1994
634.'11–dc20   94-10944
                                               CIP
                                             AC

What a great snack an apple makes!

What a great dessert
to round off a meal!

Apples are so nice and crisp
when you bite into them . . .
so tasty and juicy.

And think of all the good things to eat that are made from apples – apple pie . . . applesauce . . . apple butter . . . apple jelly.

Good things to drink, too – apple juice and apple cider.

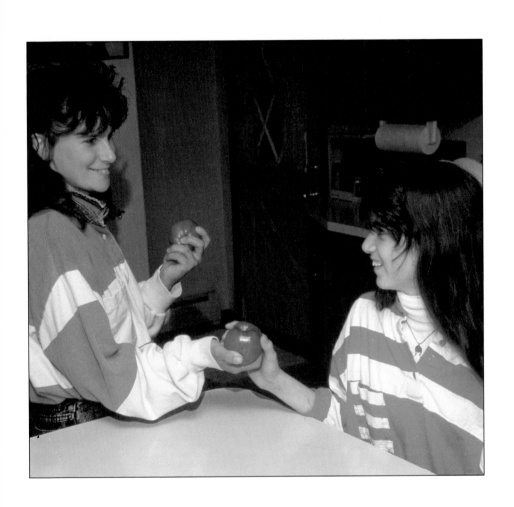

8

We like apples so much that we call a well-loved person the "apple of our eye!"

Apple trees grow in many
parts of the world.

They need rich soil,
a certain amount of
rainfall, and weather that
isn't too hot or too cold.

Some apples can be picked
during the summer.

But most of them are
harvested in the fall.

If apples are stored in cool places, they will keep fresh for a long time.

That means you can enjoy apples all year round.

If you plant a seed from an apple, an apple tree will grow.

But you can't be sure that it will bear the kind of apples you want.

So farmers have a different
way of growing apple trees
– grafting. The farmer
cuts a bud from a tree that
produces good apples.

Then he puts it into a cut
in the trunk of another
apple tree already rooted
in the ground.

He wraps the bud to the tree with tape. The new tree grows from the old tree's trunk and roots.

After about three years,
this grafted tree begins to
bear apples – good apples.

There are many different kinds of apples.

Crab apples are small
and sour, yet good-tasting
jellies are made from them.

The varieties of apples
we eat have names
like Jonathan . . .

McIntosh . . .

Winesap . . .

Granny Smith . . .

Rome Beauty.

The ones you probably
eat most often are
called Red Delicious
and Golden Delicious.

With names like those, they sound as good as they taste!

Words You Know

apples

Red Delicious

Golden Delicious

apple juice

apple pie

crab apples

Jonathan

apple trees

grafting

31

Index

About the Author

Allan Fowler is a free-lance writer with a background in advertising. Born in New York, he lives in Chicago now and enjoys traveling.

Photo Credits